Bo Diddley

Before You Accuse Me 14

Bo Diddley 18

Crackin' Up 11

Hey, Good Lookin' 24

I Can Tell 28

I'm A Man 34

Mona (I Need You Baby) 44

Pills 39

Pretty Thing 48

Ride On Josephine 54

Road Runner 59

Say Man 64

Who Do You Love 70

You Can't Judge A Book By The Cover 76

Wise Publications
part of The Music Sales Group
London / New York / Paris / Sydney / Copenhagen
Berlin / Madrid / Tokyo

Published by
Wise Publications
14-15 Berners Street, London W1T 3LJ, UK.

Exclusive Distributors:
Music Sales Limited
Distribution Centre, Newmarket Road, Bury St Edmunds, Suffolk IP33 3YB, UK.
Music Sales PTY Limited
20 Resolution Drive, Caringbah, NSW 2229, Australia.

Order No. AM995632
ISBN 978-1-84772-759-6
This book © Copyright 2008 Wise Publications,
a division of Music Sales Limited.

Unauthorised reproduction of any part of this publication by
any means including photocopying is an infringement of copyright.

Music arranged by Derek Jones.
Music processed by Paul Ewers Music Design.
Compiled by Nick Crispin.
Edited by Fiona Bolton.
Obituary by Chris Charlesworth.
Song Background Notes by Michael Heatley.
Cover designed by Michael Bell Design.
Front cover photograph courtesy of Echoes Archives/Redferns.
Back photographs courtesy of LFI and Gilles Petard Collection/Redferns.

Printed in the EU.

Your Guarantee of Quality
As publishers, we strive to produce every book to the highest commercial standards.
This book has been carefully designed to minimise awkward page turns
and to make playing from it a real pleasure.
Particular care has been given to specifying acid-free, neutral-sized paper made from
pulps which have not been elemental chlorine bleached.
This pulp is from farmed sustainable forests and was produced with special regard for the environment.
Throughout, the printing and binding have been planned to ensure a sturdy,
attractive publication which should give years of enjoyment.
If your copy fails to meet our high standards, please inform us and we will gladly replace it.

www.musicsales.com

BO DIDDLEY
(1928–2008)

Among the many legends who might be said to have invented rock'n'roll, few have a greater claim than Bo Diddley. The tough-talking, Mississippi-born guitar-singer had the singular distinction of having personally invented a wholly original rhythmic tempo, a style that in time would be appropriated by everyone from Elvis Presley and Buddy Holly to the Rolling Stones and The Who, and from Bruce Springsteen to U2, not to mention just about every fledgling guitarist who's managed to master a single chord.

It is a foundation stone of rock and is simplicity in itself, best conveyed in words by the intonation of the simple phrase 'shave and a haircut (pause) two bits'. By repeating this beat endlessly and giving it a good thump from behind by a drummer who knows his way around floor toms, even the most inexperienced of garage bands can get a crowded ballroom up on their feet and dancing in no time at all.

It made its first appearance in 1955, as the A-side to Bo's first Chess recording which he named in honour of himself, 'Bo Diddley'. It was the start of a series of self-referential songs with the same rhythm, all hammered out without a single chord change, all of them delivered with down-home wit and sexual innuendo, all performed lustily on a home-made rectangular red guitar, vocals and rhythm bathed in echo, the reverberation amplified and distorted. Accompanying him were Jerome Green, his maracas player, and The Duchess, Bo's gorgeous sister, matching the rhythm on a similarly-shaped model. It was the sound of freedom and pleasure and for all the thrills Bo's beat inspired in America's teenagers, it chilled its conservative elders to the bone.

Bo Diddley died in 2008, and although his contribution to rock history was noted by his induction into the Rock and Roll Hall of Fame in 1987, the second year of its inception, he never felt he was truly rewarded for bestowing his gift upon the world. He continued working to the last and was deeply suspicious of anyone who might seek to profit from his work. "I tell musicians, 'Don't trust nobody but your mama,'" he said in an interview with *Rolling Stone* in 1995. "And even then, look at her real good."

Bo was born Ellas Otha Bates in McComb, a small town about 15 miles from the Louisiana border, and was reared by his mother's cousin, Gussie McDaniel. When the family moved to Chicago, his name was changed to Ellas McDaniel. He studied violin from the age of seven to 15 and started playing guitar at 12, on an acoustic model given to him by his sister. He worked as a carpenter and mechanic, and also took up professional boxing, but began a musical career playing on street corners with friends and with a band called the Hipsters who became the Langley Avenue Jive Cats.

In 1951, Bo landed a regular spot at the 708 Club on Chicago's South Side, with a repertoire influenced by Louis Jordan, John Lee Hooker, and Muddy Waters, and in late 1954, he teamed up with harmonica player Billy Boy Arnold, drummer Clifton James and bass player Roosevelt Jackson. In 1954 Diddley made a demo record with the Jive Cats which came to the attention of Phil and Leonard Chess who took them into the studio. They re-recorded the songs—'Bo Diddley' and 'I'm A Man'—at Chess with a backing ensemble comprising Otis Spann (piano), Lester Davenport (harmonica), Frank Kirkland (drums) and Jerome Green (maracas). The record was released in March 1955, and 'Bo Diddley', became a No. 1 R&B hit.

It was around this time, or maybe just before, that Ellas McDaniel became Bo Diddley. There are various schools of thought on how the name came about. Some say it was thought up by Billy Boy Arnold, while others point to a one-stringed instrument called a Diddley Bow, often simply a length of wire stretched between two nails hammered into a wooden door. Whatever its genesis, the name became his trademark in songs such as 'Bo Diddley's A Gunslinger', 'Diddley-Daddy', 'Hey Bo Diddley' and many more.

For all his originality, Bo found the going hard in the early part of his career. He fell foul of Ed Sullivan in 1955 for playing 'Bo Diddley' instead of the requested 'Sixteen Tons' on Ed's Sunday night showcase. Afterwards Sullivan told Bo he wouldn't appear on TV again, and he didn't play a network show for ten years. In attempts to capitalise on teenage fads, Bo was obliged to swallow his pride and make twist and surf records in the early sixties which failed to sell.

In the event he was rescued by a British following that emerged after he was discovered in the early part of the decade by the Rolling Stones, who featured several of his songs in their repertoire. 'Mona' was a highlight of their first 1964 album which led to it being covered by scores of groups, while their third single (and first major hit), 'Not Fade Away', though strictly speaking a Buddy Holly cover, owed absolutely everything about it to the Bo Diddley beat. The Pretty Things named themselves after one of his songs and other Diddley songs were covered by The Yardbirds, The Animals, Manfred Mann, the Kinks and the Downliners Sect. When Bo toured the UK for the first time in 1963, he was given a hero's welcome.

It took longer for his star to rise in America and when it did, it was largely due to another of his staples, 'Who Do You Love', which was covered in concert by The Doors and thence picked up by Bob Seger and Tom Rush. In the UK, the progressive band Juicy Lucy had a No. 14 hit with the same song in 1970.

However, the list of performers who have co-opted the Bo Diddley beat for their own songs is virtually endless, and includes Elvis Presley ('His Latest Flame'), Johnny Otis ('Willie And The Hand Jive', also covered by Eric Clapton), The Who ('Magic Bus'; they also played Bo's 'Road Runner' live), David Bowie ('Panic In Detroit'), The Stooges ('1969' & '1970'), Bruce Springsteen ('She's The One'), U2 ('Desire'), The Smiths ('How Soon is Now'), and The White Stripes ('Screwdriver').

Bo remained sanguine about all this but never forgot that he was the man who started it all. Like almost all the musicians from his era, he was paid a flat fee for his recording and never received any royalties, let alone monies from those artists who copied his beat. "I am owed. I never got paid," he said in the nineties. "A dude with a pencil is worse than a cat with a machine gun."

In any event, he was obliged to take work other than being a musician. He spent many years in New Mexico as a law officer and served for two and a half years as Deputy Sheriff in the Valencia County Citizens' Patrol; during that time, he personally purchased and donated three patrol cars. For the remainder of his life he resided in Archer, a small farming town near Gainsville, Florida, where he attended church with some of his children, grandchildren and great-grandchildren. Bo continued to tour around the world as the decades passed by, often on the revival circuit, and wherever he went he was revered by those who recognised the huge contribution he made to 20th-century music, including his disciples, the Rolling Stones, who featured him as a special guest during a prestigious New York date on their 1989 Steel Wheels tour.

Bo Diddley died from heart failure aged 79, and at his funeral in Gainsville, he was celebrated as a musical legend. As the church filled up with his many relatives and musical peers, the choir began a refrain of "Hey Bo Diddley" with the crowd responding in kind. The flowers around the casket included two arrangements in the shape of square guitars, and so vast were they, that they almost obscured the pulpit. A two-hour musical celebration followed the funeral, and in the days that followed, many musicians stepped forward to pay tribute to the bespectacled genius.

Mick Jagger: *"He was an enormous force in music, a wonderful, original musician… an enormous influence on the Rolling Stones."*

B. B. King: *"His legacy will live on forever. We will never see his like again. He was a music pioneer with a unique style. We always had a good time when we played together."*

Robert Plant: *"His voice and relentless glorious anthems echo down through my years. The royal shape shifter continues to influence four generations of musicians on a daily basis."*

Eric Burdon: *"I've been a fan of his since 16, 17 years of age—probably one of the first records I ever bought. I call it bone music because it goes to your bone. I copied the jacket he was wearing for my first major TV appearance in England."*

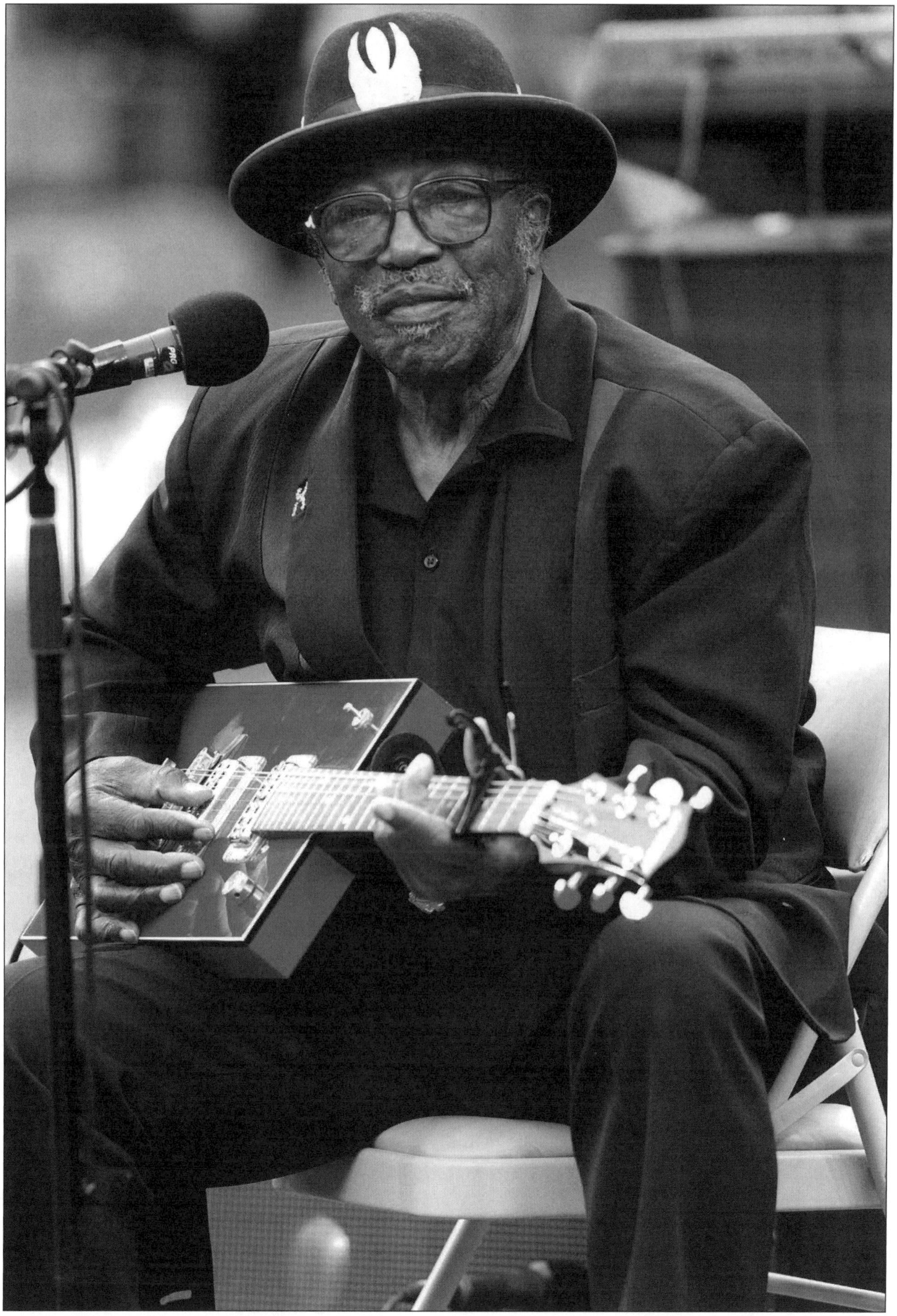

Slash: *"He's a huge hero of mine and the fact that he knew who I was is a huge compliment. Bo Diddley created a myth that was uniquely his own. An entire rhythm is owed to one guy and that's pretty rare."*

Crackin' Up

Words & Music by Ellas McDaniel

The summer of 1959 saw Bo make his first appearance in the Billboard Hot 100 with this song, which peaked at No. 62. It featured him playing his recently adopted rectangular-shaped guitar which, as ever, made the early running before being joined by maracas and vocal. Just two minutes and six seconds long, 'Crackin' Up' made its point—a complaint against a nagging wife/girlfriend—with admirable economy. These early songs were arranged for guitar, voice, tom-toms and maracas, with no cymbals and no bass, proving that less can often be more when it comes to music.

E
F#m7
B
E
al - ways hol - ler - in' 'bout where I've been._ (Ooh,
(2.) do your laun - dry and your cook - ing too._ (Ooh,
3° Instrumental
F#m7
B
E
F#m7
B
ooh.) You're al - ways scream - in' 'bout the mon - ey I spend._
ooh.) What for a wo - man can a man like me do?_
E
F#m7
B
E
(Ooh, ooh.) What's bug - gin' you? (Yeah,
(Ooh, ooh.) You're bug - gin' me. (Yeah,
F#m7
B6
E
F#m7
B
Play 3 times
yeah. You're crack - in' up.) 2. I
yeah. You're crack - in' up.) 4. I
3

spoiled you wo-man, a long time a-go. (Ooh, ooh.) I used to cook your meals and bring to your door. (Ooh, ooh.) I'm all bit-ter. (Yeah, yeah, you're bug-gin' me.)

Repeat ad lib. and fade

Before You Accuse Me
(Take A Look At Yourself)

Words & Music by Ellas McDaniel

Originally concealed on the B-side of the single 'Hey Boss Man' in 1957, 'Before You Accuse Me' gained a new lease of life when Eric Clapton adopted it as one of his stage favourites. (Having first encountered it as a Yardbird, he made it a highlight of 1992's Grammy Award-winning *Unplugged* album.) Creedence Clearwater Revival also took a shine to the song and included it on *Cosmo's Factory*. The song starts as a conventional country blues before the stumbling guitar adds a note of dissonance that gives Diddley's original performance its own character—suitably so, given the bitter instruction to 'take a look at yourself'.

© Copyright 1957 EMI Longitude Music/Figure Music Incorporated, USA.
EMI Music Publishing (WP) Limited.
All Rights Reserved. International Copyright Secured.

-fore you ac-cuse me take a look at your-self.

You say I've been spend-ing my mon-ey on oth-er wo-men,
Well, now you say I been run-ning 'round, but
% Well, now you say I've been buy-ing oth-er wo-men clothes,

but you been run-ning with some-bod-y else.
you've got some-bod-y else.
you been tak-ing mon-ey from some-bod-y else.

1. I

E
A
E7
called your Ma-ma 'bout three or four nights a - go.
2° Instrumental
A
I called your Ma-ma 'bout three or four nights a -
E7
B
- go. Well, your Moth-er said, "Son, don't
A
E
N.C.
B
Play 3 times
call my daugh-ter no more." Be -

3. Come on back home, ba - by,___ try my love___ one more time.___

Come on back home, ba - by, try my love___ one more time.___

Well, now you been gone a - way so long,

I'm gon-na lose_____ my mind.

D.S. and fade

Be-

Bo Diddley

Words & Music by Eugene McDaniels

Few artists write a song with their name in the title, but Bo can be excused as his chosen appellation is so onomatopoeic. Leonard Chess, boss of his record label, suggested he rewrite 'Uncle John', one of the songs on his first demo tape, to showcase his new identity and a classic was born. It became his debut single in 1955, and the first of at least a dozen songs that celebrated his own legend including 'Bo Diddley's A Gunslinger', 'Diddley Daddy' and 'Bo's A Lumber Jack'. He played it on *The Ed Sullivan Show* a year before Elvis Presley appeared on the same programme, while Buddy Holly not only covered the song but arguably plagiarised it for his own song, 'Not Fade Away'.

Bo Did-dl-ey buy ba-by a dia-mond ring.

© Copyright 1955 Arc Music Corporation.
Jewel Music Publishing Company Limited.
All Rights Reserved. International Copyright Secured.

If that dia-mond ring___ don't shine,___

he gon-na take it to a pri-vate eye.___

If that pri-vate eye___ can't see,

he bet-ter not take the ring___ from me.

Bo Did - dl-ey caught a nan - ny goat,_____ to

make his pret-ty ba-by a Sun-day coat.

Bo-Did-dl-ey caught a bear-cat, to

make his pret-ty ba-by a Sun-day hat.

G

_____ you come to my house and rack that bone?_____
Look at that Bo-do, oh, where's he been?_____

Won't_

I take my ba-by all the way from home.
Up your house and gone a - gain.

1.

2.
Bo Did-dl-ey, Bo Did-dl-ey, have you heard? My

Repeat ad lib. and fade

pret - ty ba-by said she was a bird.

Hey, Good Lookin'

Words & Music by Chuck Berry

No relation to Hank Williams' country song of the same name, this cover of Chess Records labelmate Chuck Berry's song gave Bo his second and last UK chart hit in March 1965. It also titled an album which, sadly, failed to emulate the single's popularity. The guitar style which powers 'Hey, Good Lookin''—scratchy rhythmic patterns played on a few strings at a time—was a result of playing his first instrument, the violin. As his fingers were too big to move around the fretboard easily, he tuned the guitar to an open E chord and moved a single finger up and down.

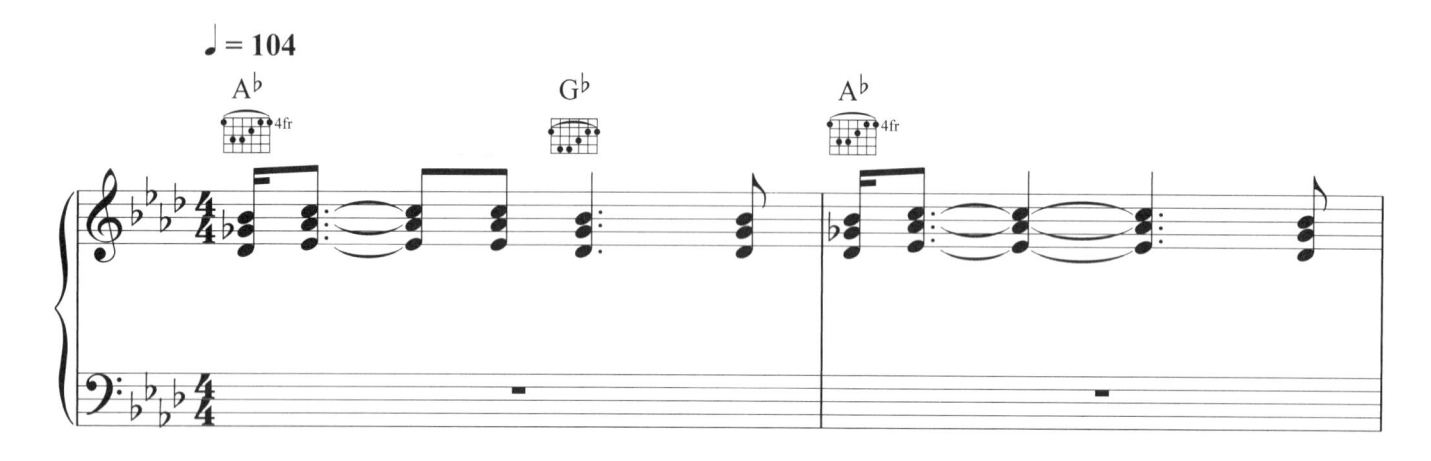

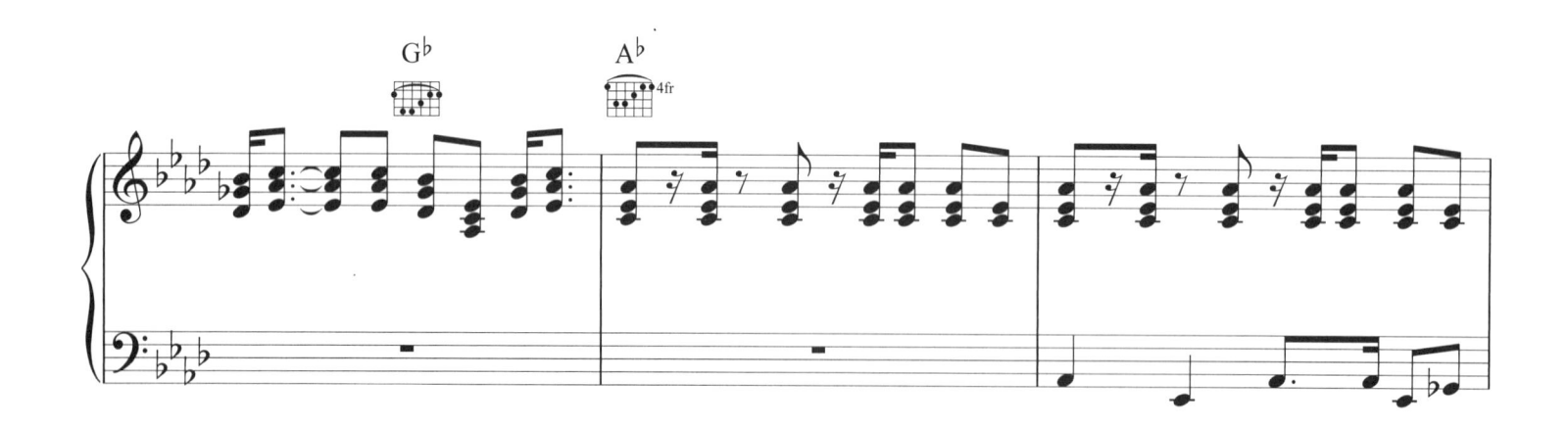

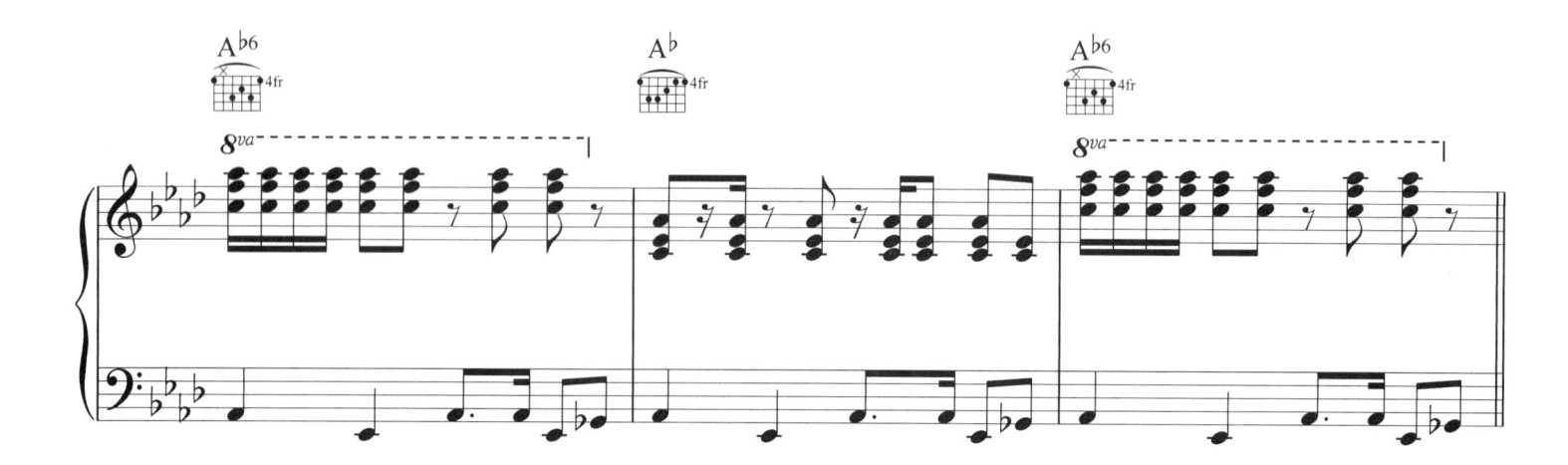

© Copyright 1962 Arc Music Corporation.
Tristan Music Limited.
All Rights Reserved. International Copyright Secured.

A♭
4fr
A♭6
4fr
1. Hey, Good_ Look - in'.
2. Hey, Good_ Look - in'.
3° Instrumental
8va
Hey Good_ Look - in'. Done
Hey Good_ Look - in'. Done
made Bo Did - dl - ey your mar - shall man._ Done
Bo Did - dley soon gon - na be in town._ His
3
dep - u - tise_ Bo Did - dl - ey's band._ They got a
dep - u - ty boys_ gon - na track you down._

twi-light pos-se look-in' for you. They sent a
He got a let-ter by Po-ny Ex-press, 'bout a

A. P. P. and a road-block too.
girl who's plan-ning on meet-ing him chest to chest.

Play 3 times

4. Hey, Good Look-in'.
5. Hey, Good Look-in'.
6. Hey, Good Look-in'.

Hey, Good Look-in'. Done
Hey, Good Look-in'. He
Hey, Good Look-in'.

A♭
4fr
A♭6
4fr
3
Bo Did-dl-ey 'bout to find his quail. He like a
drawn Matt Dil - lon and Chest - er too. The
3° Instrumental
8va
hound dog hunt-ing on his lone - ly trail. As
wrath of man he e-ven out - drew.
soon as you hear his gui - tar's tune you
When you hear the beat of that there drum you
3° Repeat and fade
bet-ter sur-ren - der and it bet-ter be soon.
bet-ter be work - ing out when he come.

I Can Tell

Words & Music by Samuel Smith

Recorded in 1962, 'I Can Tell' was typical of the songs of the time in finding a readier audience in Britain, where R&B was taking off in a big way, than in his home country where black artists and the blues were considered passé. When, two years later, a reporter asked John Lennon what he was most looking forward to seeing in America when he got there, his two-word answer, 'Bo Diddley', came as a surprise. The Beatle would have known that British band Johnny Kidd and the Pirates covered 'I Can Tell' and used it as the B-side to 'A Shot Of Rhythm And Blues' in its year of original release, the single being quickly flipped to showcase the stronger song.

© Copyright 1962 Arc Music Corporation.
Jewel Music Publishing Company Limited.
All Rights Reserved. International Copyright Secured.

1. I can tell__ be-cause it's plain to see.__
(2.) asked your Ma - ma and your Pa - pa too.__
(3.) you won't an - swer your tel - e - phone.__

I can tell__ the way you look at me.__
What more can a poor man do?__
When I knock on your door they say that you ain't home.

The way you know,   you hold my hand.   Yes, pretty baby, I can understand.

Now, you've been runnin' with a heart-breaker, Charlie Brown. Yes, I knew 'bout that you put me down.

Your sister let me in and tell me I can wait. When you come home you show up real late.

I can tell. I can tell.

I know you don't love me no more? No more.

2° Instrumental

No more. No more.

Oh, no more.

I can tell, oh, I can tell.

G
N.C.
1.
2.
D.S. al Coda
I know you don't love me no more. 2. I
3. Well,
Coda G
I said no more.
1.
2.
G
No more.
4. Ba - by I can give you
ro - mance,

on-ly if___ you give me an-oth-er chance.

C

I'll cook your food and__ wash your clothes.__

G

I prom-ise to__ keep you warm__

D.S.S. and fade

when it gets cold._____ I___ can

33

I'm A Man

Words & Music by Ellas McDaniel
Arranged by Bo Diddley

Originally the B-side of 'Bo Diddley', 'I'm A Man' has become a classic in its own right in the hands of bands like the Yardbirds. It received an unexpected 'cover' by fellow Chess artist Muddy Waters, but since he was the song's inspiration Bo couldn't really complain too much when he 'stole' it back and called it 'Manish Boy'. The diminutive title was Waters' riposte to his younger rival! In recent years 'I'm A Man' has been voted the Greatest Blues Song in an internet poll by an American website, beating stiff competition in B. B. King's 'The Thrill Is Gone', Robert Johnson/Magic Sam's 'Sweet Home Chicago' and Elmore James/Stevie Ray Vaughan's 'The Sky Is Crying'.

1. Now, when I was a little boy, at the age of five, I had something in my pocket, keep a lot of folks alive.

© Copyright 1957 Arc Music Corporation.
Jewel Music Publishing Company Limited.
All Rights Reserved. International Copyright Secured.

2. Now I'm a man,_____ May twen-ty - one,_____ you know ba - by, we can have a lot of fun.
3. All you pret - ty wo - men, stand in line,_____ I can make love to you, ba - by, in an hours time.
4. I'm go - ing back down, to Kan - sas to_____ bring back a sec-ond cou - sin, Lit - tle John The Con - que - roo.

I'm a man._____ I spell M._____ A._____

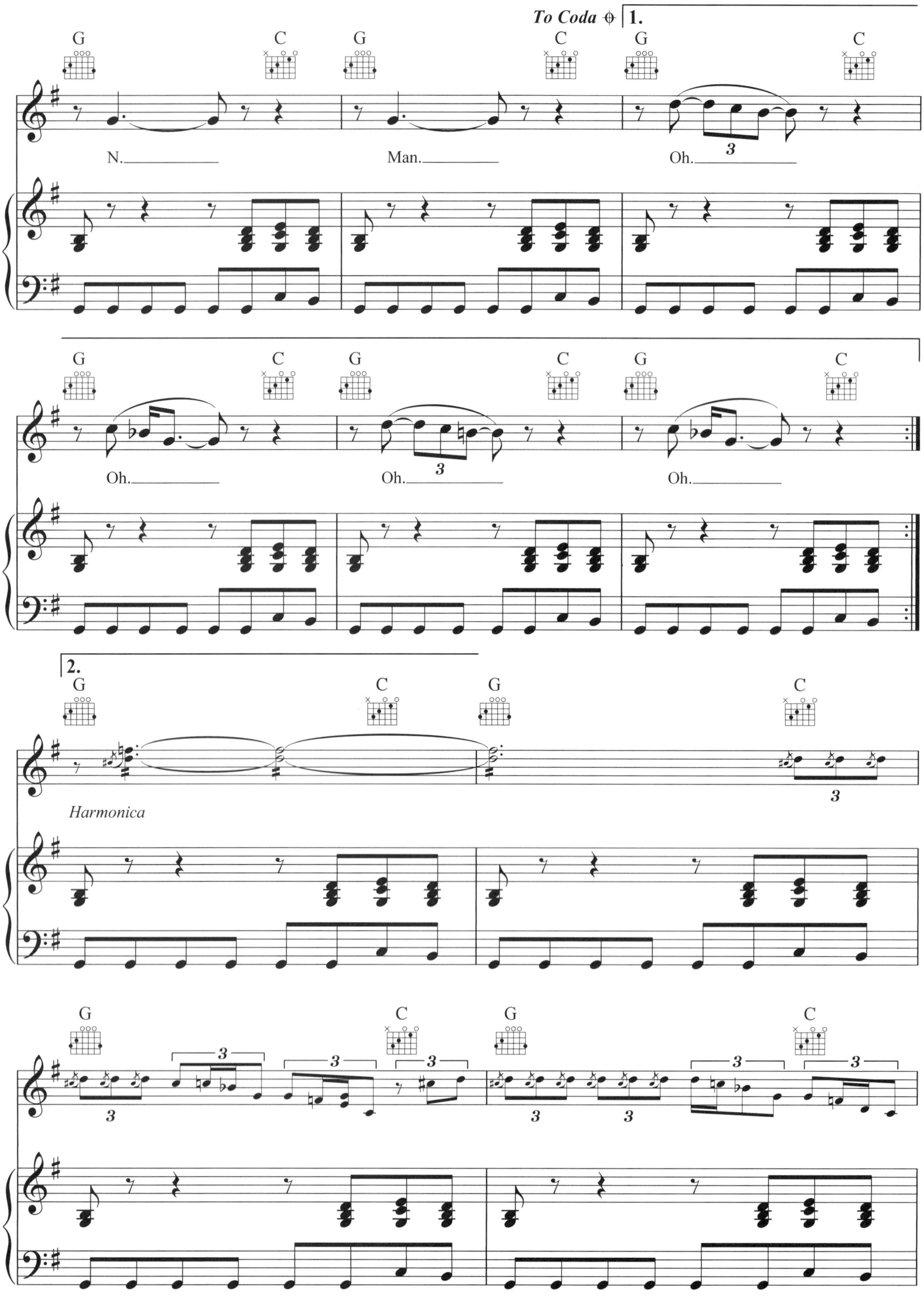
To Coda
1.
G C G C G C
N.
Man.
Oh.
Oh.
Oh.
Oh.
2.
Harmonica

D.S. al Coda

Oh.____ Oh._____

Oh.____ Oh._____

5. The line I shoot will nev-er miss.

G C G C G C
The way I make love to 'em, they can't re-sist. I'm a man.
G C G C G C
I spell M. A. N.
G C G C G C
Man. Oh. Oh.
G C G C
Repeat and fade
Oh. Oh.

Pills

Words & Music by Ellas McDaniel

Even before hanging out with the Clash, Bo Diddley had become a new-wave icon thanks to proto-punks the New York Dolls. They appropriated 'Pills', originally recorded at Bo's home studio in Washington, DC, in 1961, as an anthem of their own and covered it on their eponymous debut album in 1973. Ex-Dolls guitarist Johnny Thunders revisited the main riff to 'Pills' when he cut the punningly titled 'Too Much Junkie Business', but sadly life imitated art when he overdosed in 1991. Bo, of course, remained hale and hearty, touring incessantly until shortly before his sad demise in June 2008.

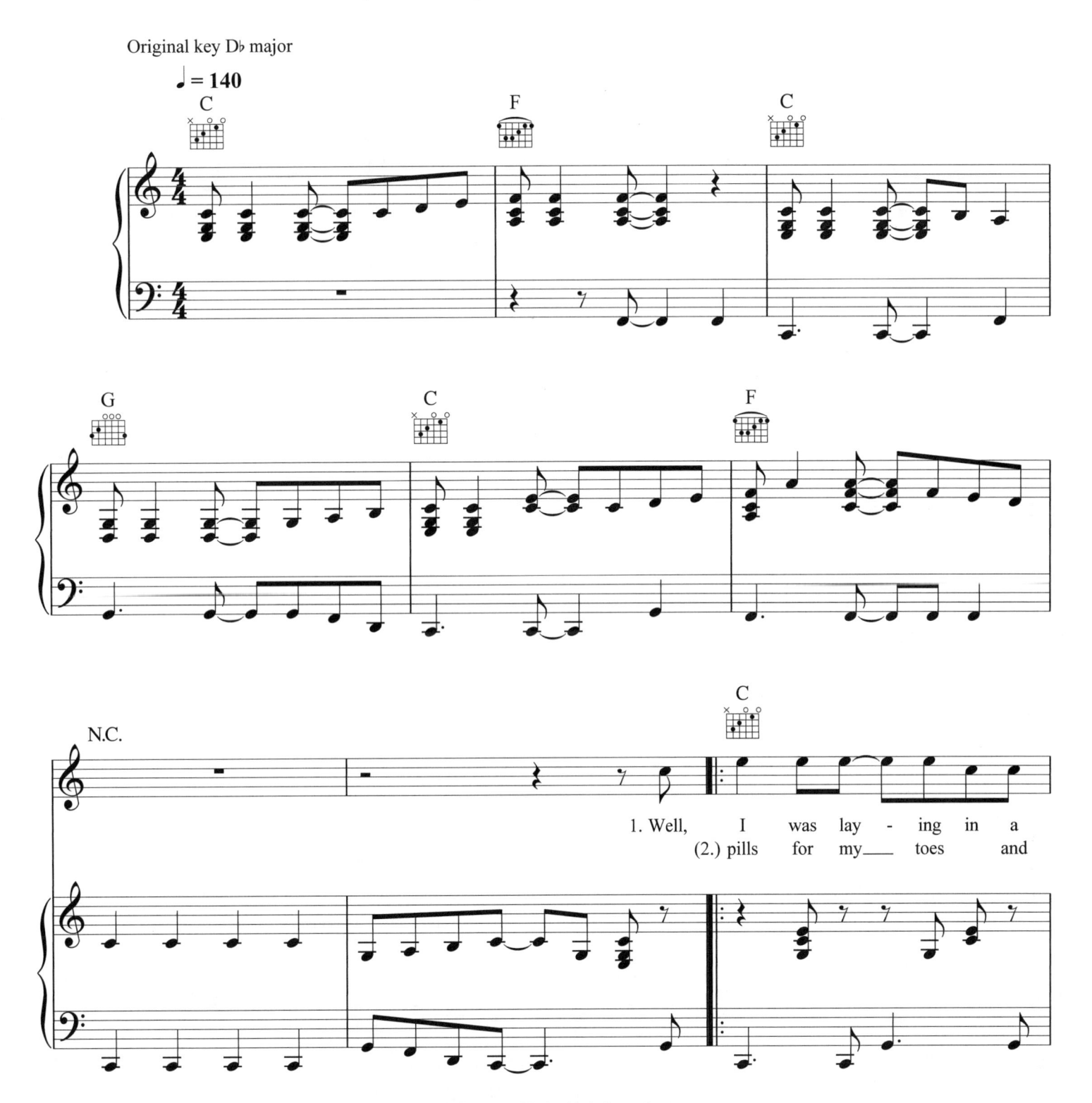

Original key D♭ major

♩ = 140

1. Well, I was lay-ing in a
(2.) pills for my toes and

© Copyright 1964 Arc Music Corporation.
Jewel Music Publishing Company Limited.
All Rights Reserved. International Copyright Secured.

hos - pi - tal bed, a rock 'n' roll nurse went to my head. Says,
they did-n't ache. She gave me pills for my love but a lit-tle too late. She gave me

"Hold out your arm and stick out your tongue, I got some pills boy, I'm gon'
pills for my heart that put me at ease. The rock 'n' roll nurse shook me

give you one." } She went to my head, to my head,
dead to my knees.

to my head, to my head. She went to my head,

to my head.___ Well, I was lay - ing in a hos - pi - tal bed.___

2. She gave me

3. Nur - ses, nur - ses, can't you see, I don't dig this jive you giving to me. You give me a pill, you give me a shot. You got me won-d'rin what, what have I got. It went to my head, to my head,

4. Doc - tor doc - tor, run, you see, I don't dig this jive this nurse giving me. She give me a shot, she give me a pill. I'm tak-ing this junk a-gainst my will. She went to my head, to my head,

to my head,__ to my head.__ To my head,__ she went

2° (He went)

to my head.__ Well, I was lay - ing in that hos - pi - tal bed.__

Repeat and fade

Mona
(I Need You Baby)
Words & Music by Ellas McDaniel

British audiences first came across 'Mona' in June 1964 when it reached No. 42 in Bo's own hands. Amazingly it fared better a quarter of a century later when Aussie soap star-turned-singer Craig McLachlan took it to No. 2 in the summer of 1990. But the most intriguing cover was recorded by the Clash during the *London Calling* sessions in 1979, the same year Bo appeared as their opening act. 'I can't look at him without my mouth falling open,' a star-struck Joe Strummer said during the tour. But did Joe know 'Mona' was a song of praise written for a 45-year-old exotic dancer who worked at the Flame Show Bar in Detroit?

© Copyright 1964 Arc Music Corporation.
Jewel Music Publishing Company Limited.
All Rights Reserved. International Copyright Secured.

Mo - na._ 1. Tell you Mo - na what I wan - na do,_ build my house_ next door_ to you._ Can I see you some - time?_ We can blow kiss-es through_ the blind._ Can you come out in the front?_ Lis - ten to my heart go bum-pe-ty bump._

45

I need you ba - by, that's no lie. With-
-out your love I would sure - ly die.
G
Hey,
Mo - na.
Oh,
Mo - na.
Hey, hey, hey, hey,
Mo - na.
Oh,

Mo - na.

Hey, Mo - na. Oh, Mo - na.

D.S. and fade

Pretty Thing

Words & Music by Willie Dixon

It took Bo Diddley until 1963 to reach British shores, and his tour with the Everly Brothers and the Rolling Stones will live long in the memory of anyone who witnessed it. The Stones dropped the Diddley covers from their set in respect for their idol, while former Stone Dick Taylor was so impressed that he decided to call his new group The Pretty Things. Mixing Bo's chugging, muted-string style of guitar playing with liberal harmonica interjections, spiritual, sanctified rhythms and what Bo called 'the feeling I have of making people (want to) shout', songs like this helped lay the foundations of 1970s funk.

© Copyright 1955, 1983 Hoochie Coochie Music (BMI) administered by Bug Music Limited (70%)/
Arc Music Corporation/Jewel Music Publishing Company Limited (30%).
All Rights Reserved. International Copyright Secured.

let me buy you a wed-ding ring, let me
hear the choir sing. Oh, you pret-ty
E
thing. 2. You pret - ty thing,
let me walk you down the aisle. Darl-ing,

wear a love-ly smile. Oh, you pret-ty thing.

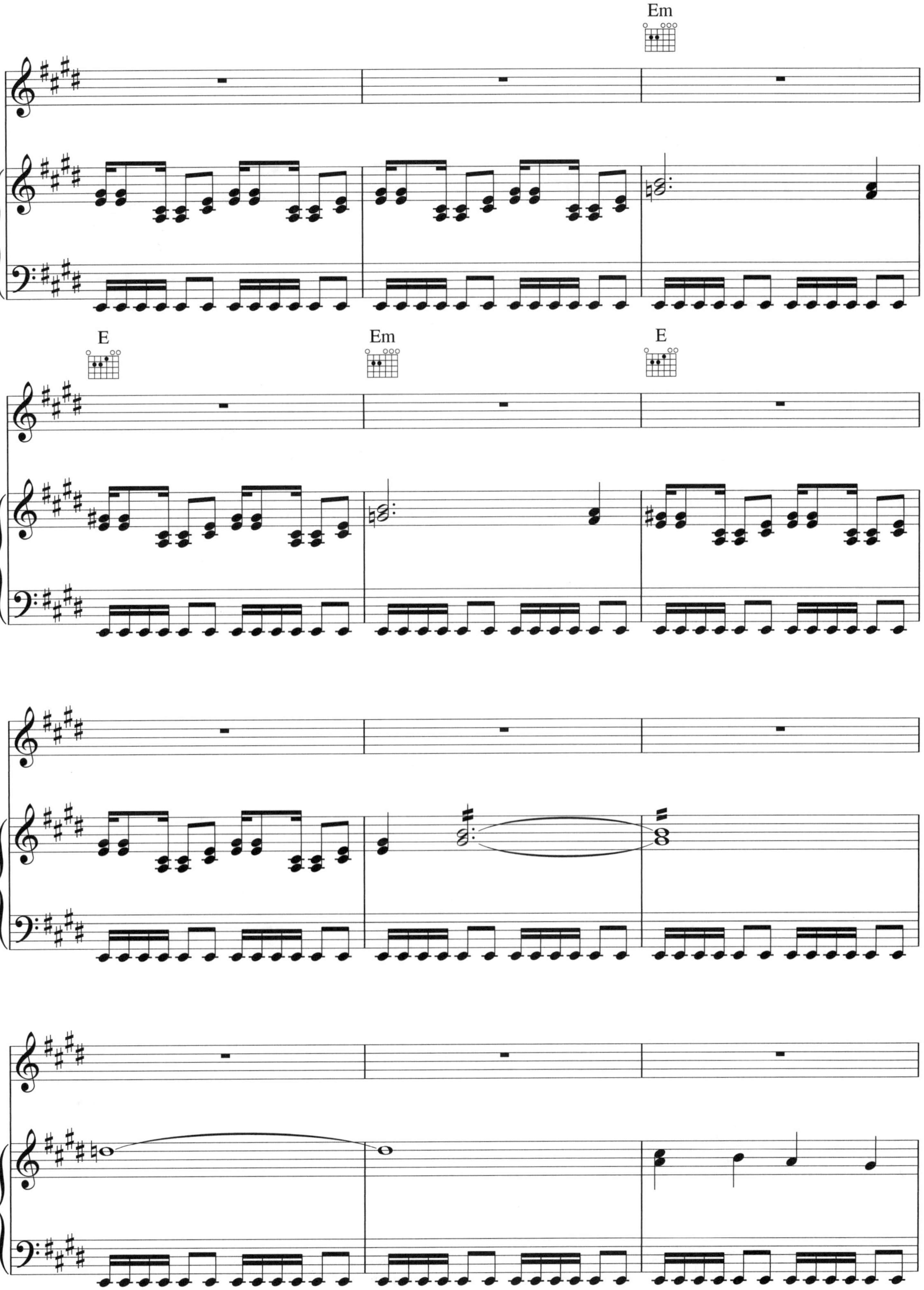
Em
E
Em
E

3. Let me kiss you gentle, squeeze and hold you tight.

Let me give you all my love, the rest of my life.

4. You

pretty thing.
5. Pretty thing.
Let me hold you by my side,
Let me dedicate my life.

and become my blushing bride.
You will always be my wife.

1. You

2.
pretty thing.

D.S. and fade
Oh, you pretty thing.

Ride On Josephine

Words & Music by Ellas McDaniel

A key track on the 1961 album *Bo Diddley Is A Gunslinger*, the original heavily features the maracas of pal Jerome Green and shares the automobile theme so beloved of Chuck Berry, with whom Bo often recorded and toured. The song was covered by white blues guitarist and singer George Thorogood & The Destroyers 16 years later. Thorogood also based his 'Bad To The Bone' hit on Diddley's patented rhythm, but while Diddley was bitter at those who'd profited from his work—'I opened the door for a lot of people, and they…left me holding the knob', he told *The New York Times* in 2003—he forgave and forgot when George asked him to appear in his video!

© Copyright 1961 Arc Music Corporation.
Tristan Music Limited.
All Rights Reserved. International Copyright Secured.

G

Ride on___ Josephine, ride___ on.

D

Ride on___ Josephine, ride___ on.

G   **C**

Ride on___ Josephine. You got a runnin'___ machine. Baby, baby,

G   **D7**   **G**

ride on___ Josephine, baby ride on.   1. Well___ Jo-

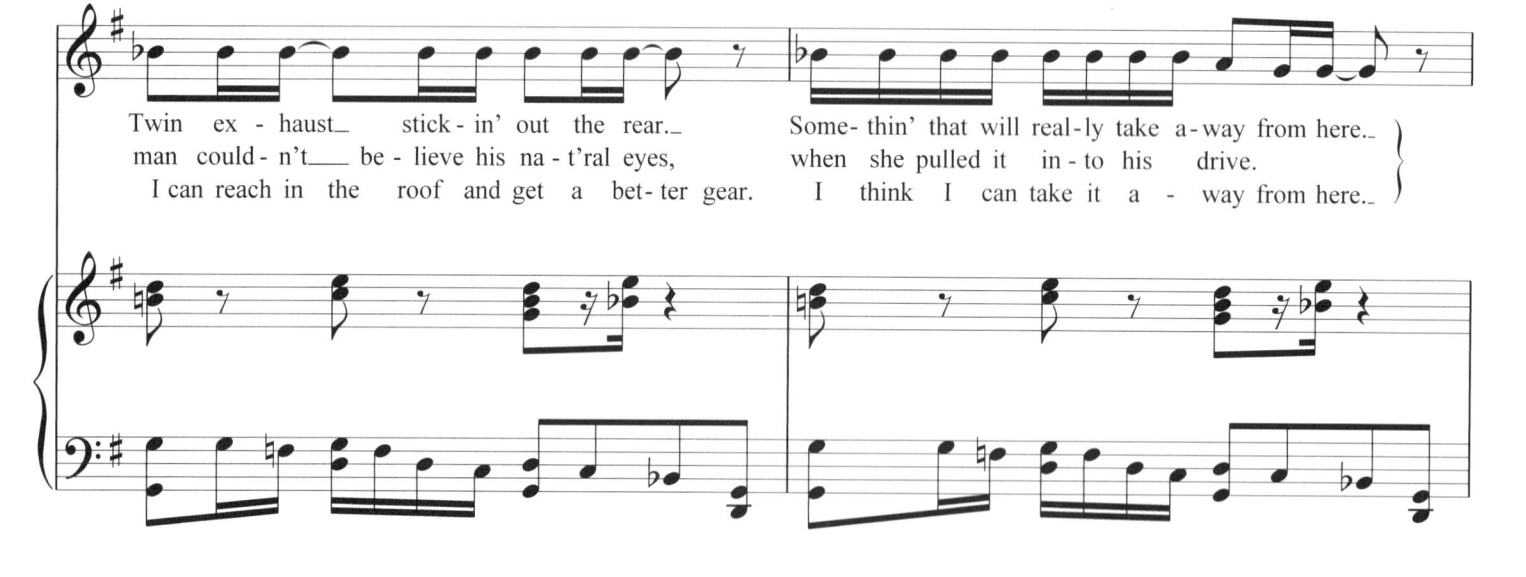

-se-phine driv-in' a hot rod Ford, twin car-bu-ret-tor will eat up the road.
2. Jo-se-phine's Ford be-gin to run hot, she tried to trade it in at a used car lot. The
(3.) for-ty eight Cad-il-lac with Thun-der-bird wings, tell-in' you ba by, it's a run-nin' thing.

Twin ex-haust stick-in' out the rear. Some-thin' that will real-ly take a-way from here.
man could-n't be-lieve his na-t'ral eyes, when she pulled it in-to his drive.
I can reach in the roof and get a bet-ter gear. I think I can take it a-way from here.

Ride on Jo-se-phine, ride on.

2° Spoken: Said,

D
Ride on Jo - se-phine ride on.
Josephine,
Josephine
G
C
Ride on Jo - se - phine. You got a run - nin' ma - chine. Ba - by, ba - by,
child,
your tank is leaking gas!
1.
2.
G
D7
To Coda
G
G
ride on Jo - se - phine, ba - by ride on.
Say what?
Baby, you better shut up and come on ride with me.
Yeah, you'd better ride with me.

You say I'd better mind my buisness? *Ha, ha, ha, ha!* *You got business baby, you, you good business!* *I just love good business.* *You get what kind of car I'm drivin'?* *Well, I'm* *I'm a* *3. I'm drivin' a*

D.S. al Coda

Coda

on. *Vocal ad lib.*

Repeat ad lib. and fade

Road Runner

Words & Music by Ellas McDaniel

Bo Diddley kicked off the 1960s with 'Road Runner', a straight 12-bar blues that remains one of his best known and most frequently covered songs. It was, suitably enough, the opening track on the Pretty Things' eponymous first album in 1965, and was more recently immortalised by Aerosmith on their 2004 covers album *Honkin' On Bobo*. Less well known is the fact that it was also the first piece of music played by Keith Moon as drummer with The Who. The 'Road Runner' of the title was a cartoon character created by animation director Chuck Jones in 1948 for Warner Brothers whose catchphrase, 'Beep Beep', features in the lyric.

© Copyright 1959 Arc Music Corporation.
Jewel Music Publishing Company Limited.
All Rights Reserved. International Copyright Secured.

(Beep beep!) I'm a road run-ner hon-ey, and you can't keep up with me. (Beep beep!) I'm a road run-ner hon-ey and you can't keep up with me. (Beep beep!) Come on, lets race.

Ba - by, ba - by, you will see.

Spoken: Here I come!

(Beep beep!)

Move over honey.

Drums

(Beep beep!)   *Let me by.*   (Beep beep!)

Move over, baby.   (Beep beep!)   *Let this man by.*

61

E
B
B♭
(Beep beep!)
Oh yeah, how am I doin'?
I'm gonna show you baby, look out your head.
A
N.C.
E
Gonna put some dirt in your eyes. (Beep beep!)
Here I go!
E
(Beep beep!)
(Beep beep!)
(Beep beep!)
Take my hand baby.
fast.
I wanna prove to you that I'm a
Ha ha ha ha ha!
(Beep beep!)
(Beep beep!)
(Beep beep!)
a road running man.
But it don't look like you gonna last.
Goodbye!

A7
E
(Beep beep!)
(Beep beep!)
(Beep beep!)
I wanna show you something,
that I'm the
fastest in the land.
I've got to
put you down.
B
B♭
A
N.C.
Now let me by.
(Beep beep!)
I'll see you some day,
ba-by somewhere hanging around.
1.
E
Oh, yeah!
(Beep beep!)
You say you
2.
E
Repeat and fade
N.C.
E
N.C.
E
(Beep beep!)
(Beep beep!)

Say Man

Words & Music by Ellas McDaniel

It took five years for Bo Diddley to make the US Top 20, and 'Say Man' was the track that did it in the summer of 1959. Unusually it was based on some comic stage-style jive talking with long-time friend and fellow musician Jerome Green over his now familiar 'shave and a haircut, two bits' rhythm. The vocal had to be carefully edited for public consumption, as it's said the original would never have won airplay; lines like, 'You look like you been whooped with the ugly stick!' were apparently the tip of the iceberg! In many ways this was a precursor of the rap phenomenon that was to dominate black music in future years, and certainly it is one of the first spoken-lyric records to chart. A sequel, 'Say Man, Back Again', was less successful.

Say man...

(What's that boy?)   *I wanna tell you 'bout your girlfriend.*   *(What about my girl?)*

© Copyright 1959 Arc Music Corporation.
Tristan Music Limited.
All Rights Reserved. International Copyright Secured.

Well, you don't look strong enough to take the message.   *(I'm strong enough.) I might hurt your feelings.*

(My feelings are already hurt by being here with you!)   *Well,*   *I was walking*

E♭7

down the street with your girl the other day (Ah ha)   *And the wind was blowin' real hard.*
street with your girl.) Yes.   *(I took her home, for a drink, you know.) Took her*

E♭

(Is that right?)   *And the wind blew her hair into my face.*   *(Ah ha)*
home? (Yeah, just for a drink.) Oh.   *(But that chick looked so ugly she had to sneak up on the glass to get a*

You know what else happened? *(What happened?)* *The wind blew her hair into her face. (Yeah?) And we*
drink of water.) *Ha ha ha ha!* *You got the nerve to call somebody*

went a little further. *You wanna hear the rest of it?* *(I might as well.)* *The*
ugly. *Why, you so ugly,* *the stork that brought*

wind blew her hair into the street! *(Hey, since you told me*
you in the world ought to be arrested. *(That's alright.*

about my girl I'm gonna tell you 'bout yours. *I was walking down the*
My Mama didn't have to put a sheet *over my head so sleep could slip up on me!)*

E♭

Hey, look a - here   (What's that?)   Where you from?   (South America)   What's
Hey, look here.   (What's that?)   I been tryin' to figure out what you is.

loco

that? (South America)   You don't look like no South American to me. (I'm still from South America)
(I already figured out what you is!)   What's that? (You that thing I throw peanuts at.)   Ha ha!

E♭7

What part? (South Texas!)   Ha ha ha!

Well, look

Where are your workin' boots at?
(I got 'em on.)
Those aren't
here.
(What's that?)
You should be ashamed of
yourself.
(Why?)
E♭
6fr
no boots you got on, they broguettes.
Calling people ugly.
(I didn't call you ugly.)
What you say? (I said you was ruined, that's all.)
You
E♭7
6fr
E♭
6fr
know something? (What?)
You look like you been whooped

with the ugly stick!   *Ha ha!*   *(Hey, I ain't got nothin'*

to do with this, but I beat the fellah right.)

E♭7

Repeat ad lib. and fade

Who Do You Love

Words & Music by Ellas McDaniel

With its references to barbed wire, cobra snake neckties and human skulls, Diddley's voodoo-esque 'Who Do You Love' was far and away his most menacing lyric. This gave it great appeal to a new generation of US acts ranging from Quicksilver Messenger Service through to The Doors and Bob Seger, all of whom played it live, while Juicy Lucy took their supercharged version of the song into the UK Top 20 singles chart in 1970. The original, recorded in 1956, can be heard under the intro credits to the Ritchie Valens biopic *La Bamba*, **which was screened in 1987, the year Bo was inducted into the Rock and Roll Hall of Fame.**

© Copyright 1957 Arc Music Corporation.
Tristan Music Limited.
All Rights Reserved. International Copyright Secured.

1. I walk forty-seven miles of barbed wire. I use a cobra snake for a necktie. I got a brand new house on the roadside made from rattle-snake hide. I got a brand new chimney

Night was dark but the

made on top, made out of a hu-man skull.__ Now
sky was blue. Down the al-ley an ice-wag-on flew.

come on take a lit-tle walk with me Ar-lene and tell me, who_ do you love?_
Hit a bump and some-bod-y screamed. You should've_ heard just

what I seen. Who do you love?__

Who do you love?__ Who do you love?__

To Coda ⊕

Who do you love?___ Who do you love?___

A♭

2. Tomb-stone hand and a grave yard mind. Just twen-ty two and I don't___
(3.) -round the town, used a rat-tle - snake whip. Take it eas-y Ar-lene. Don't

D♭/A♭ **A♭**

___ mind dy-ing.⎫
give me no lip.⎭ Who do you love?___

Who do you love?___ Who do you love?___

Who do you love?___   3. I rode a-

Play 3 times ad lib.

D.S. al Coda

Coda
A♭
D♭/A♭
A♭
4fr
Ar - lene took me by the hand, she said ah - ooh - eeh, Bo, you know I
un - der - stand. Who do you love? Who do you love?
Who do you love?
Repeat ad lib. and fade

You Can't Judge A Book By The Cover

Words & Music by Willie Dixon

The double A-side single 'You Can't Judge A Book By The Cover'/'I Can Tell', released in 1962, made No. 48 in Bo Diddley's homeland. It has since been covered by The Fabulous Thunderbirds, while even TV's *Desperate Housewives* borrowed it as an episode theme, though without a guest appearance from Bo! Penned by Chess Records' bassist and house songwriter Willie Dixon, it boasts one of the classic opening verses in popular music, effortlessly rhyming tree with bee, mother with cover. But, as ever, it's that uniquely jagged instrumental style that hammers home the message. As Bo Diddley himself remarked, 'I play guitar like a drum!'…so looks can deceive after all.

Original key A♭ major

𝅗𝅥 = 116

can't___ judge an ap-ple by look-ing at___ a tree.___ You
(2.) can't___ judge sug-ar by look-ing at___ the cane.___ You
(3.) can't___ judge a fish by look-ing in___ the pond.___ You

© Copyright 1962, 1990 Hoochie Coochie Music (BMI) administered by Bug Music Limited (70%)/
Arc Music Corporation/Jewel Music Limited (30%).
All Rights Reserved. International Copyright Secured.

can't judge hon-ey by look-ing at the bee. You
can't judge a wo-man by look-ing at her man. You
can't judge right from look-ing at the wrong. You

can't judge a daugh-ter by look-ing at the moth-er.
can't judge a sis-ter by look-ing at her broth-er. You
can't judge one by look-ing at the oth-er.

can't judge a book by look-ing at the cov-er. Oh,

can't you see oh, you've
3° you

G
mis - judged me? I
can't judge me.
D
C
look like a far - mer but I'm a lov - er.
G
N.C.
To Coda II
To Coda I
Can't judge a book by look - ing at the cov - er, oh.
G
Vocal ad lib.

Play 3 times ad lib.

D.S. al Coda I

2. You

Coda I G

Vocal ad lib.

cov - er.

3. You

Repeat ad lib. and fade